I0704972

Reviews from Readers

Pictures for my mother with dementia. She loves birds.

-*Mary Sapp*

50 THINGS TO KNOW ABOUT BIRDS IN MISSOURI

Birds to Watch in the Show Me State

Stephen L. Reinbold

50 Things to Know About Birds in Missouri Copyright © 2024 by CZYK Publishing LLC. All Rights Reserved.

All rights reserved. No part of this book may be reproduced in any form or by any electronic or mechanical means including information storage and retrieval systems, without permission in writing from the author. The only exception is by a reviewer, who may quote short excerpts in a review.

Cover designed by: Ivana Stamenkovic

Cover Image: 1. By William H. Majoros - Own work, CC BY-SA 3.0, https://commons.wikimedia.org/w/index.php?curid=16066775

2. By Rhododendrites - Own work, CC BY-SA 4.0, https://commons.wikimedia.org/w/index.php?curid=77559329

3. By Sasata - Own work, CC BY-SA 3.0, https://commons.wikimedia.org/w/index.php?curid=11477259

4. By Peter Trimming from Croydon, England - 'Tutoke'Uploaded by snowmanradio, CC BY 2.0, https://commons.wikimedia.org/w/index.php?curid=15975742

5. By John Harrison, CC BY-SA 3.0, https://commons.wikimedia.org/w/index.php?curid=6038070

6. By Alan D. Wilson, www.naturespicsonline.com - http://www.naturespicsonline.com/ (higher resolution version obtained in correspondence with website owner), CC BY-SA 2.5, https://commons.wikimedia.org/w/index.php?curid=1214891

7. CC BY-SA 3.0, https://commons.wikimedia.org/w/index.php?curid=774888
8. By gary noon - Flickr, CC BY-SA 2.0,
https://commons.wikimedia.org/w/index.php?curid=4077294
9. By Casey Klebba - Own work, CC BY-SA 4.0,
https://commons.wikimedia.org/w/index.php?curid=72255655

CZYK Publishing Since 2011.
CZYKPublishing.com
50 Things to Know

Lock Haven, PA
All rights reserved.

ISBN: 9798345731352

50 THINGS TO KNOW ABOUT BIRDS IN MISSOURI

BOOK DESCRIPTION

You have heard of the St. Louis Cardinals, but is the Cardinal the state bird of Missouri? Do you want to know what bird seen by Lewis and Clark in Missouri is no longer living today?   Of birds introduced to Missouri, do you want to know which ones have been harmful?

If you answered yes to any of these questions then this book is for you...

Fifty Things to Know About Birds in Missouri by Stephen L. Reinbold offers an approach to bird lore in the state of Missouri that most books on birds of the Show-Me-State overlook. They tell you how to identify the birds and that is all. Although there's nothing wrong with that, based on knowledge from the world's leading experts, there are surprising answers to these and other questions about Missouri's feathered creatures.

In these pages you'll discover the largest, the smallest, the fastest, the tamest, and the most unusual avian species. This will help you appreciate how varied and wonderful the natural history of the state really is.

 By the time you finish this book, you will know the answers to the above questions and many more, so grab YOUR copy today. You'll be glad you did.

TABLE OF CONTENTS

8. Black-capped Chickadee

9. Peregrine Falcon

10. Ruby-throated Hummingbird

11. Bald Eagle

12. Snowy Owl

13. Indigo Bunting

14. Least Tern

15. Whooping Crane

16. Northern Cardinal

17. Song Sparrow

18. Purple Martin

19. Barn Swallow

20. Barn Owl

21. Kildeer

22. Sora Rail

23. Mourning Dove

24. American Robin

25. Black Vulture

26. Red-tailed Hawk

DEDICATION

The author would like to dedicate this book to his sister Keturah who first took him on walks in the woods to show me and encourage me in my love of nature.

ABOUT THE AUTHOR

Stephen Reinbold has a Masters Degree in Zoology and a Ph.D. in Biological Sciences and taught college biology classes for thirty years before retiring. He has always been a student of nature and has traveled and photographed animals and plants in Missouri, where he has lived for thirty years, and at least ten other states. He has continued traveling, reading, and writing after retirement. In addition to scientific curiosity, he maintains a sense of awe and stewardship toward the wonderful creation that we have inherited. He is currently meeting with old and young alike and in-person and virtually who want to develop mutual interests in understanding and enjoying the gift of our living world.

INTRODUCTION

"I observed a great number of Parrot queets [parakeets] this evening."

William Clark, June 26, 1804

1. EASTERN BLUEBIRD

Sorry, Cardinal! You got your name on St. Louis's baseball jerseys, but the honor of state bird of Missouri goes to the delightful little Eastern Bluebird. It is the state bird of New York also. This striking bird has a beautiful blue back, wings, and tail; it has an orange neck and sides, and a white belly. The song is a whistled *chiti WEEW wewidoo* and the call a musical *jeew*. With its attractiveness, it has generally fared well along-side humans, as it prefers the more open forests of suburbs or orchards near human habitation, and it helps control insects. However, the alien House Sparrows and Starlings that accompanied us invaded the small tree cavities where the non-aggressive Bluebird nests. Fortunately, we have compensated by giving our worthy state bird little nest boxes with small openings and our careful diligence to keep them in house and home. The Eastern Bluebird, like its fellow member of the thrush family, the American Robin, is often viewed as a harbinger of spring. The Iroquois believed that the Bluebird would scare off Sawiskera or Flint, the spirit of winter. However, either bird may be seen in winter in more southern parts of its nesting range. Where does the blue color come from? See the tip for Indigo Bunting below.

2. MISSOURI'S PARAKEET

Actually, it was called the Carolina
Parakeet, but this beautiful bird lived over
much of the United States, from as far west as
Colorado to the eastern seaboard and Gulf
Coast. For explorer William Clark on the
eponymous Lewis and Clark Expedition, it
would have been no surprise to see the birds

on the present-day site of Kansas City, Missouri. However, within a little over one hundred years, the species was extinct. Incredibly, Incas, the last Carolina Parakeet, died in the same cage in the Cincinnati Zoo in 1918, where four years before, Martha, the last Passenger Pigeon died. Even a stuffed and mounted specimen allows you to appreciate its green body, bright yellow head, and reddish orange face. And, like the Passenger Pigeon, they were estimated to be very numerous at one time, even millions of birds, and then became extinct rapidly. Like the pigeons, they were decimated by deforestation, hunted for feathers or food, persecuted for protection of crops, and burdened by behavior that made them flock together. Ironically, they were desired as pets and valued for eating cockleburs, noxious weeds, that not only are unpleasantly prickly, but are actually poisonous to most animals, including cats that happened on the birds' carcasses. Such stories have been all too common when human beings do not have the foresight to see where their behavior leads. This viewpoint led to extinction of the Great Auk, the Dodo Bird, the Heath Hen (eastern subspecies of Prairie Chicken), and Ivory-billed Woodpecker.

3. EURASIAN TREE SPARROW

Why mention the Eurasian Tree Sparrow in a book about Missouri birds? Meet the well-behaved cousin of the very unpopular House Sparrow. The Eurasian Tree Sparrow was introduced to the St. Louis area in 1870. This attractive, unobtrusive, cavity-nesting and neat little bird has slowly moved out around the city up and down the Mississippi River. They feed mostly on seeds, including those of some weeds. A cursory glance of birders' lists will show that the bird is frequently sighted in the St. Louis area, but it has not spread widely. The Eurasian Tree Sparrow male has a chocolate brown crown and a black spot in the middle of its white cheek, unlike the duller and larger male House Sparrow. Make no mistake, bird or other introductions of non-native species is a practice that threatens native wildlife, just as the House Sparrow did. The House Sparrow, for example, drove the Eastern Bluebird out of its nesting sites, as noted above. In the particular case of the Eurasian Tree Sparrow, an urban-tolerant bird was introduced with relatively benign effects.

4. GREATER ROAD RUNNER

Road Runners in Missouri? "I have seen the Warner Brothers cartoon" you may say, "and I was distinctly under the impression it took place in Arizona or somewhere like that." True, but the Greater Roadrunner does indeed live in the southwest corner of the Show-me State, where it dashes through low brush chasing lizards and snakes. Roadrunners elevate their tails and bushy crests excitedly and are natural entertainers and might qualify as Missouri's most unusual bird. It belongs to the cuckoo family after all. The Greater Roadrunner is a gray and brown bird with yellow eyes, and standing 23 inches it is larger than a crow. And, like crows, it is noisy and non-musical. It flies only reluctantly. The southwestern counties in Missouri have desert-like habitats called *glades* where rocky soil and southern exposure give rise to aridity, supporting cactus and other xeric plants, along with desert animals, such as horned lizards ("horned toads"), rattlesnakes, tarantula spiders, and scorpions. There is a clearinghouse for bird sightings in Missouri that is continually updated by bird watchers online. Greater Roadrunners have been sighted already this year in Blue Eye in Stone County on January 22 and at Saddle Rock in

Christian County on February 26. The Greater Roadrunner lives throughout the southwestern United States. And, yes, there is a Lesser Road Runner that lives in Mexico.

5. GREATER PRAIRIE CHICKEN

And speaking of Greater, the Greater Prairie Chicken lives in parts of Missouri's northern and western prairies, but the species is highly endangered due to the loss of native tall grass prairies to the plow. Prairie remnants have survived on poor land, cemeteries, and railroad rights-of-way, especially where burning or mowing have prevented growth of woody vegetation and introduced weeds. Prairie restoration has been promoted by the Missouri Department of Conservation and by universities throughout the Midwest. Although prairies are protected in many areas, the Prairie Chickens still struggle to survive. There are many predators on the eggs and young. Even so, one was sighted as recently in Missouri as last year on November 3, at Pawnee Prairie in Harrison County. The spring breeding season is the best time to see them. The chicken-sized male inflates yellow-orange throat sacs and erects feather "horns" during mating season in the spring. The male birds put on a spectacular visual and auditory display of dancing and booming to attract as many females as possible. The male then loses interest and leaves the females to make a nest, incubate the eggs, and raise the young. The dozen or so tiny hatchlings follow her, but must learn to feed on their own immediately. These grouse-like birds feed on seeds and insects and nest on the ground. The Greater Prairie Chicken is found in scattered remnants of tall grass prairie from the Great Lakes to eastern Oklahoma and from the Canadian prairies south to Texas, being scattered along the Gulf Coast. The Lesser Prairie Chicken lives to the southwest in the central plains with drier prairies of western Oklahoma, Kansas, and Texas.

6. SCISSOR-TAILED FLYCATCHER

The Scissor-tailed Flycatcher is unmistakable. The male's black and white tail hangs down in two long plumes while perching, usually on a tree, a fence, or on a utility wire. The female is close beside. Like all Flycatchers, they fly with acrobatic grace and capture flying insects on the wing. The Scissor-tailed Flycatcher is a bird of open areas, and its nesting range is surprisingly restricted to the southern plains, only Texas, Oklahoma, Kansas, Nebraska, and western Missouri. For Missouri residents who are birdwatchers, a trip to the western part of the state to open country with available perches, where these birds are easily seen, is a must. The Scissor-tailed Flycatcher and most other members of the flycatcher family spend the winter in the tropics. Fortunately for me, a pair of the birds routinely each summer claimed an area just across the parking lot from where I taught biology for 27 years. They disappeared for a few years, likely because of the construction of a housing and commercial development across the street, but came back again last year. I never saw more than a single pair of them on campus; they are aggressive toward other birds like the closely related Kingbirds. The similar-looking Fork-tailed Flycatcher has an even longer tail that is all black although only occasionally wanders into Missouri, last e-bird record on 28 April 2009 in Buchanan County.

7. SNOW GOOSE

At Squaw Creek National Wildlife Refuge
(now called Loess Hills NWR) along the
Missouri River in northwest Missouri in
November through March, be prepared to be
awed. Thousands of Snow Geese rest here
between winter refuge farther to the south and
nesting far to the north in the arctic tundra. A
small number will usually stay here through

the winter. Called the Snow Goose because of being nearly all white, there is also a dark form of the same species, formerly considered a different species, called the Blue Goose, but dark and light birds both are white under the wings and on the head. There are many intermediate variations as well. In March, a few years ago, I was able to take many photographs of Snow Geese. Needless to say, there was lots of loud honking and cackling. They are very important game birds in northwestern Missouri, so expect the towns to fill up with hunters in March, so you might plan to arrive a little early.

8. BLACK-CAPPED CHICKADEE

The little Black-capped Chickadee comes to feeders for seeds and suet (fat) during the winter. They can become so tame that they will take seeds from your out-stretched hand. In the summer these little birds often hang upside down from twigs while feeding on insects. The winter flocks break up in summer for the nesting season, and the birds become much less conspicuous. The bird almost identifies itself by its voice or call—*chick-a-dee-dee-dee.* It can be confused with the higher-pitched call of the slightly smaller Carolina Chickadee, but the two mostly have divided their geographic ranges. The Carolina lives south of Chesapeak Bay and the Ohio River and southwest through southern Missouri to Oklahoma, and the Black-capped north of that ambiguous east-west line, through northern Missouri, and all the way to the west coast. The little Black-capped Chickadee is at home in the deciduous forests (and suburban yards) of the eastern states and north to the primarily coniferous forests in Canada, and ranges all the way west to Alaska. The Black-capped Chickadee, of course, has a distinct black cap and also a black throat or bib, which strongly set off the white face or cheek. The rest of the feathers are gray with white trim on the wings. Unlike many species of birds, males and females look alike. Both are about five to six inches long. The two leave the winter flock in spring to make or modify a cavity in a dead tree where they incubate six to eight speckled brown eggs. The summer diet consists mostly of small insects which they find on their own, making them far less dependent on humans who were expecting them at feeders.

9. PEREGRINE FALCON

Like the Bald Eagle, the Peregrine Falcon almost succumbed to the insidious effects of the insecticide DDT in the 1970s. The insecticide concentrated upward through the food chain to the ducks and geese that were the favored prey of this incredible bird. The Peregrine Falcon flies high over its prey and makes a spectacular dive or "stoop" at over

200 miles per hour, the fastest flight of any bird, to dash its prey to the ground where it is dispatched. Fortunately, discontinued use of DDT allowed these birds to recover. Peregrine Falcons mostly nest far to the north in the high arctic or western mountains and winter on the coasts. Now some of the birds nest on city skyscrapers, including downtown Kansas City where they hunt pigeons. The Peregrine Falcon has dark facial markings, a black "mustache," and dark top of the head or "hood." In the Old World as well as the New, the Peregrine Falcon has been trained by falconers to hunt birds and mammals. Interestingly, female falcons are larger than males, and they are preferred by falconers. Its total length may be 21 inches, and its wingspan is 40 inches. Traditionally, all the day-hunting, large, predatory birds were

grouped in the same order, but that question is unsettled. The falcons are placed in their own family—the Falconidae. They are all fast flyers with pointed wings that appear swept back, like a jet's wings. None of them soar, as do the hawks, eagles, and vultures.

10. RUBY-THROATED HUMMINGBIRD

The tiny Ruby-throated Hummingbird is the smallest of Missouri's summer visitors. The male has an iridescent red throat, and both male and female are metallic green above and white below. This diminutive bird hovers and buzzes over flowers, inserting its long, slender beak and equally long tongue to dine on nectar. Humming birds must fly to the tropics in the winter. They love sugared water offered at special feeders, but please do

31

not tempt them to linger in the fall or it may get too cold before they reach the winter refuge. Instead, welcome them again next summer! Then they will build a tiny carefully woven nest where they will incubate two tiny eggs. Although the only hummingbird to nest in Missouri, a few others may occasionally pass through. Green Violet-ear from Mexico is larger, nearly all green, with some violet on face and tail. Anna's from the west coast is also a little larger with some red on crown and throat and distinctive white eye-ring. Remarkably for such tiny birds even others have been seen--Calliope, Broad-tailed, Allen's, Rufous, and Black-chinned--all within the last 16 years, mostly in the fall.

11. BALD EAGLE

The Bald Eagle is Missouri's largest bird, standing at 31 inches, with wings spanning 80 inches, and weighing over 9 pounds. (Actually, Golden Eagles weigh slightly more, but are rarely seen in Missouri, being a more western bird and less associated with water.) Endangered by the potency of the insecticide DDT in the 1970s, that impaired successful reproduction, the Bald Eagle and other large raptors nearly disappeared in the lower 48 states. The Endangered Species Act has brought the Bald Eagle back to allow them, not only to be winter visitors, but now to nest in Missouri. I have seen the huge nests along the Missouri River in northern Missouri where they are provided with an assortment of prey, including migrating waterfowl and the fish they catch or steal or scavenge. Of course, they are not really bald, but the head is covered with white feathers in adults after a progression of molts leading to their fourth year. Otherwise, they have mostly dark brown plumage as seen in profile. The adult also has a distinctly yellow beak with a strong hook. Eagles spend most of their air time in soaring on thermal updrafts which lighten their load. They hold their wings flat unlike the golden eagle or most hawks which are bowed up or down. Their tail is also distinctly white underneath. They have relatively weak voices.

12. SNOWY OWL

We had a very cold early February in Missouri this year. The polar air must have pushed ahead of it an arctic bird, the Snowy Owl, seen here on rare occasions. They are unmistakable, being almost entirely white and very large. They nest in the arctic tundra where they feed on rodents and large birds. Perhaps due to seasonal or longer cycles in their prey populations, they fly far to the south, especially when the arctic is exceptionally cold. One was spotted not so far from me, at Kansas City International Airport in Platte County, on January 6 this year. Harry Potter's owl Hedwig is a Snowy Owl. Although the fictional owl was a female, her part was played by male Snowy Owls in the movies. The actor playing Harry had to wear thick gloves to avoid serious injury from some of the world's most powerful talons, effective against large birds and rabbits. Owls of course have sparked the human imagination, being associated with wisdom for centuries, at least since the time of the ancient Greeks.

13. INDIGO BUNTING

Like the Eastern Bluebird discussed above, the Indigo Bunting is a striking blue. Indigo refers to a plant and the dark blue dye that comes from the plant of the same name that was once grown as a major crop in the southeastern states. Interestingly, there is no blue dye or pigment in the feathers of the Indigo Bunting or Bluebird or any other bird. The purplish, blue color of the male is said to be a structural color; that is, it comes from the arrangement of keratin, the same substance as in fingernails, that makes up the feathers. The keratin is arranged in very thin layers that are evenly spaced at a microscopic level, so that each layer serves as a mirror. The distance between layers is such that blue, and even more so, ultraviolet light, is maximally reflected. Light waves of certain lengths are superimposed by a succession of mirrors, so that wave piles on wave, much as ocean waves might do. The result is that we see the birds as blue, at least in bright sunlight. The birds themselves see the ultraviolet light, having an additional cone type in their retinas that we lack. It is not certain how the birds use this ability.

14. LEAST TERN

The Least Tern is endangered in Missouri.
Least Terns nest in colonies on gravely or
sandy islands in large rivers. Now they are
mostly restricted to the Mississippi south of
St. Louis, but formerly nested on the Missouri
and other rivers in the state. Although this
may seem a precarious habitat on which to
lay two or three buff, lightly spotted eggs,
historically rivers ran low in the summer

nesting season providing many such islands for these tiny birds only 8-10 inches tall. They have a black cap, and gray back, tail fork, and wings; otherwise, plumage is white, including the forehead that sports a yellow bill with black tip. However, river flows are tightly controlled by the Army Corps of Engineers for several, often incompatible, purposes. For the Missouri this control comes mostly from upstream reservoirs in the Dakotas and Montana. The citizens of those states want to maintain high reservoir levels in the summer to promote fishing which is compatible with tern nesting downstream. However, in Missouri, commercial interests want to keep water levels high enough in the Missouri River during summer for barge traffic. Also, farmers want spring floods stopped by maximizing upstream reservoir capacity in the spring. But the water has to be released sometime. For farmers, summer release is part of rebuilding capacity to hold next spring's floods. Releasing the water in the fall would allow the birds to be long gone by then to Mexico or South America.

15. WHOOPING CRANE

Another unusual sighting in Missouri this year was the highly endangered Whooping Crane that was seen in Saint Mary in Saint Genevieve County on January 29. It is North America's tallest bird at over four feet and is white except for black wing tips. The only natural colony of the birds, numbering only about two dozen a century ago, spends its winters in Texas and nests in Canada. However, the Missouri bird may have been headed to Wisconsin. That state has been tested as a potential back-up nesting area for bringing the Whooping Crane back from its current low numbers. Relying on the strong, instinctive drive to migrate and to imprint on older, parental birds for protection, Whooping Cranes artificially hatched in Wisconsin were imprinted on tiny aircraft which they learned to follow. In this case, they were led to Florida as a second potential wintering area. They flew back to Wisconsin in the spring, and there is hope that they will learn a new migration pattern that will persist for generations. Some of the Cranes have lingered in midwestern states, including Missouri, and may even spend the winter farther north than the Gulf Coast. Overall, there may be as many as 600 birds currently, including both the natural and newly established populations.

16. NORTHERN CARDINAL

The Northern Cardinal is the state bird of more states than any other—North Carolina, Virginia, West Virginia, Kentucky, Ohio, Indiana, and Illinois. Also, many sports teams are named for this bird, such as the St. Louis

Cardinals baseball team and their minor league Memphis Redbirds. ("Redbird" is a common name for this bird.) Growing up in Illinois where it was the state bird, I have long identified with the "Redbird." Now, living in Missouri, I keep a painting on my wall of a pair of Cardinals depicted in winter. Indeed, a pair of the living birds frequently winters about my house. They add cheer on gloomy days. This beautiful bird is a year-round resident in the East and Midwest and a frequent visitor for sunflower seeds at winter feeders. It is unmistakable with its bright red plumage and crest. The female is duller but with reddish tinge. The area behind the beak is black, while the beak itself is red. It derives its name from the vestaments of the official in the Roman Catholic Church. The short, conical beak readily crushes seeds—the primary food of these birds. The voice consists of a song *What cheer cheer cheer. . . purty purty purty.* Cardinals belong to the huge order of perching birds and are related to Grosbeaks, not surprisingly, another bird with a stout beak—all mostly seed eaters. In the spring a pair of cardinals builds a deeply concave nest in a tangled location hidden in branches where they lay three or four light green eggs. The pair is rarely separated. Both sexes sing year-round and the males are particularly aggressive, erecting the crest as a threat toward other males. Males are said to be a little duller during nesting season, perhaps to be less conspicuous around the nest. The only other bird that closely resembles them is the elegantly named Pyrrhuloxia, which lives in the Southwest, and tends toward gray, not bright red. Bright red makes the cardinal a target for predators, including bird-eating hawks and small mammals, such as domestic cats. Squirrels may eat the eggs.

17. SONG SPARROW

Madge madge madge, put-on-your-tea-kettle-ettle-ettle is the beautiful song of the Song Sparrow, a New World sparrow, not to be confused with the Old World sparrows that include the House Sparrow. This one has a heavily streaked breast as do many members of the family and a large dark spot on the breast. It is a year-round resident in the upper

Midwest, but also nesting farther north and west and wintering farther south as well. It lives in many habitats as long as there is undergrowth where it can conceal its nest of grass lined with hair. Three to six brown-spotted green eggs are tended by the parents. It is the most common of our sparrows and lives compatibly with humans.

18. PURPLE MARTIN

Purple Martins prefer open land, including farms and residential areas. They nest over most of the U.S. east of the Rockies and west of the Great Basin on the Pacific coast. Although they nest in trees with lots of woodpecker holes in the wild, humans have encouraged them for their very effective eating of flying insects for hundreds of years, going back to Native Americans who hung out hollow gourds to encourage them to nest near their gardens. European Americans followed suit with multi-compartmental bird houses because of their colonial nesting preference. Here they make a grassy nest and incubate four or five white eggs. They winter in the tropics, for their diet cannot be sustained in the northern winter. John James Audubon, nineteenth century American naturalist and artist, wrote that Martin houses could be found at many country taverns, and he chose accommodations for the night by how well the proprietors' provided for the birds. The nest boxes do take care, however. I remember my neighbor going through the laborious process of taking down the long pipe with the cumbersome housing complex in the fall, cleaning it, and putting it back up in the spring, but not so early as to give the sparrows or starlings a chance to get started.

19. BARN SWALLOW

For Swallow nest construction effort, I always admired the sturdy, mud houses under the protective eaves of a barn that Barn Swallows make. Barn Swallows are smaller than Martins and have a long, forked tail and blue-back body with orange breast. Like the Purple Martin, they have long, pointed-wings and feed while flying, being on the wing for long periods. They rest by perching, often in family groups on a branch or utility line. They rarely rest on the ground. As consumers of mosquitoes and other insect pests, Swallows are benefactors of humans and are welcome on the farm or in the city.

20. BARN OWL

The Barn Owl stands out among the owls, being placed in its own family in the Order Strigiformes. All owls have a ruff of feathers around the eyes called the facial disk which functions to direct sound into the ear openings. The Barn Owl has a distinctive heart-shaped facial disk, whereas that of most owls is round. Owls have no external ear and the so-called ears are tufts of feathers. The tufts are called coverts. The coverts of Barn Owls are asymmetrically arranged, and the actual ear openings are such that the left is higher than the eyes and the right lower. As a result, Barn Owls have exceptional hearing, especially with regard to determining direction and distance, being able to hear mice rustling under leaves or even snow. They can hunt in complete darkness. These adaptations allow the Barn Owl to live on all continents, unlike any other owl. Although this wide distribution may currently keep them safe from global extinction, they can be locally endangered, including in the State of Missouri. Even picking up a dead one could be breaking the law.

21. KILDEER

The Kildeer is a shorebird in the Plover Family. Actually, this largest of the ringed plovers is better known as a bird of open fields, golf courses, and even gravelly parking lots. The eggs are often laid on a sandy or gravelly surface and not concealed at all well. How is the nest protected in this precarious situation? The female Kildeer, which stays with the nest, will walk away, dragging a wing, and piping out its name *kildeer* loudly. A predator will follow her with the expectation of an easy meal. Once the enemy is led to a safe distance, the instantly "healed" bird will fly away, still calling *dee dee dee* loudly. I have heard this many times, as Kildeer nest every summer in the parking lot of the campus where I taught and saw the brown and white birds with two rings across its breast. Thinking back much farther, my father, who was a farmer, but had a tender spot for birds (except House Sparrows), would lift the cultivator out of the corn field to pass harmlessly over the spotted eggs.

22. SORA RAIL

The Sora Rail is a game bird in Missouri. Rails are wading birds that prefer dense marshy vegetation which provides cover as well as invertebrates such as snails and other edibles. Although rarely eaten as are ducks and geese, the birds are hunted for sport although they are hard to find but easy to shoot. The autumn season lasts from the beginning of September to the end of

November. A few of the birds nest in Missouri at the southern limit of its breeding range, but most are seen as migrants. Missouri has many impoundments that are bordered by suitable habitat for Sora Rails where water is retained by dams or levees. The birds migrate principally to the Gulf Coast States to winter. A game management issue for Missouri is how to provide proper habitat for Sora, but concomitantly for other migratory wading and shore birds. A recent, multi-year study determined the timing of Sora migration in Missouri from northwest along the Missouri River to central and south along the highly important Mississippi flyway. Basically, the results showed a consistent beginning in the middle of August, peak in mid-September, and end in late October. Why is this important? River

. MOURNING DOVE

Mourning Doves, also called Turtle Doves, almost always found in pairs, so that we scribe devoted couples as being "lovey vey." The buff colored birds have a long bordered with white, and they are also autiful to look at. The song is a mournful *o-ah coo coo coo.* They thrive in parks and

impoundments are carefully manag
federal government and input from
is important to prevent interference
migration, such as by lowering lake
levels too soon in the fall, which ma
to create capacity to hold winter and
floods. Believe it or not, waterway
management is a contentious issue l
states up and down the rivers with c
interests. For myself, I have not see
quail-sized, grayish brown, yellow-l
birds in Missouri but did so when li
Illinois.

fields with trees and shrubs close by in our neighborhoods and throughout most of the United States. A loose nest of twigs in a tree or shrub contains the two white eggs. Unique for birds, doves and pigeons produce "pigeon milk" in their crop which is regurgitated to feed the young. Although shy, they can be photographed if one is patient,

24. AMERICAN ROBIN

One question many people might have about the American Robin is this: is there another kind of robin that is not American? I will come back to the answer in just a bit. The American Robin is one of the most familiar birds, indeed, to Americans. They nest in yards from coast to coast. Connecticut, Michigan, and Wisconsin all chose the American Robin as state bird. They are identified by gray back, black head and tail, and, of course, distinctive orange breast (duller in females). The orange or "red" breast was reminiscent of the European Robin to colonists, also called Robin Redbreast in England. However, the birds are not closely related. The American Robin is a member of the thrush family. Only the juvenile robin has a streaked or spotted breast as a give-away that it is a thrush. The American Robin is often seen hopping (they cannot walk) on grassy lawns in a tug-of-war with an earthworm, which does not pull out easily because they are anchored by stiff bristles. Besides worms, insects make most of their summer diet. The birds are not afraid to nest close to human habitations on window sills, electrical boxes, or more pristinely in trees. The parents guard three to five blue-green eggs in a concave nest made of mud, grass, and twigs, and lined with grass. Their busy call is *cheer-up, cheerily, cheer-up, cheerily.* They also make sharper, higher pitched calls when alarmed. They fly when approached but usually not far, and if you are mowing, sprinkling, or hoeing—anything that brings worms to the surface--they will soon be back. Fledglings make clumsy attempts at flight, often landing not far from the nest. They have lovely spotted breasts. For those who survive, they feast on fruits in the fall and, surprisingly, do not go far in the winter. They move into more wooded cover and form flocks. They will visit feeders at times for seeds. They will reappear again in our yards in early spring.

25. BLACK VULTURE

The Black Vulture resembles the more wide-spread Turkey Vulture in most respects, such as a featherless head, but it is a little smaller with shorter, broader wings that are held straight out instead of in a V-shape. They also have a shorter tail, white primary feathers seen under the wings, and gray feet.

The smaller bird is actually more aggressive and may drive the larger bird from carrion. They also flap their wings more and soar less than the Turkey Vulture, and are non-migratory. In Missouri the Black Vulture is found only in the south of the state, from Barry County to the Mississippi River, being especially abundant around Table Rock Lake.

26. RED-TAILED HAWK

The Red-tailed Hawk is the most common hawk over much of the United States. It belongs to a group called "Buteos." They are heavy-bodied (two feet tall with four foot wingspan) rodent eaters. They are often seen soaring or perched conspicuously on a tall tree, searching the grass for rodents. They also eat other rodent-eaters, such as snakes. The Red-tailed Hawk is distinguished by a rust-colored tail, a whitish breast, and piercing scream *keeeeeer*. Widely distributed in deciduous forest and open country, male and female remain within calling distance of each other. Two or three spotted white eggs are laid in a bulky nest of sticks in a high tree. The nests are so large as to suggest eagle's nest to the casual observer. When growing up in Illinois in mixed country of farms and forests, they were always around, summer or winter, and the same is true in Missouri.

27. ROSE-BREASTED GROSBEAK

We often think of wings as the distinctive feature of birds, and that is correct, but the beak is more related to the feeding habits of a species. The Rose-breasted Grosbeak is related to cardinals and buntings, all characterized by stout beaks adapted to seed crushing. Grosbeaks, as implied by the name, have especially large beaks. The Rose-breasted Grosbeak nests over the northeastern and central states and north into Canada. Although they winter in the tropics, they are early arrivals in the spring nesting areas, arriving in late April to early May. Larger than buntings, they are about the size of the Northern Cardinal. In addition to the large pinkish beak, the male in breeding season has a rose-red breast and black head. Juveniles and females have black and white stripes on the head and streaked breasts. In addition to weed seeds, they eat harmful insects and are beneficial to farmers.

28. WOOD THRUSH

Another outstanding feature of birds is their singing. The thrushes, as a group, are some of our most beautiful singers. Most members of the family either nest farther north or winter in the tropics and are less familiar to us. The Wood Thrush, however, nests over the eastern half of the country, preferring deeper woods than robins, with lots of undergrowth. The song is flutelike and rises to a trill or whistle. I have sought out deep woods at times, hoping to be rewarded by their song, and consider myself fortunate when I succeed. However, seeing the brown-backed, speckle-breasted bird was another matter, as they prefer to stay concealed in the underbrush. Wood Thrushes have large blackish spots on an otherwise white breast and are brown above to a rusty brown on the head. Four greenish-blue eggs are incubated in a grassy nest in the underbrush. They feed on insects. These birds unlike the familiar robin fly to the tropics in the winter.

29. GOLDFINCH

The sun is shining brightly over the edge of the woods and over large patches of weeds. There is a beautiful song *toWEE toWEE toWEEto tweer tweer tweer,* and then, as you approach, comes a frightened *ti ti ti ti ti di di di,* as a burst of yellow joins the sunlight in the sky. This is the American Goldfinch. He is yellow except for black on the wings and forehead. She has a yellowish wash over the breast, pink bill, and black on the wings. Otherwise, she is a dull grayish, brown, as are both sexes during the fall and winter. The nest is lined with down feathers, hidden in vegetation. As a nature-loving child growing up in the country with lots of weedy fields, they were part of my July experience that I would not wanted to have been without. I may not have appreciated their service in controlling weeds, but the bird called the "American Canary" earned its reputation in my childhood estimation.

30. NORTHERN ORIOLE

Of course, birds lay eggs in a nest. Some birds build more elaborate nests than others. Now, we have to admire the Northern Oriole. The nest is large and pendulous, carefully woven together and hanging from a tree branch. Few birds go to so much effort. The pair of orioles watch over four to six eggs with irregular dark markings on a gray background. Orioles feed on a surprising variety of unpopular insects including tent caterpillars and fall webworms, in spite of the strong, unsightly silk around the larvae. Northern Orioles (often called Baltimore Orioles), however, do damage some fruit crops. Another species is known as the Orchard Oriole. Both species winter in the tropics; we welcome the beautiful and industrious orioles back again to nest in the spring.

31. MALLARD DUCK

The Mallard is our best known duck and the progenitor of the domesticated duck. Easily recognizable with its green head, yellow beak, and white neck ring. They have a turquoise patch of wing feathers, including on the female, but the rest is mottled brown.

And of course, they quack. Mallards live on any body of water, year-round in Missouri, also nesting farther north and wintering farther south. She lays eight to ten greenish eggs in a grassy nest hidden in vegetation. Mallards far outnumber other ducks and are abundant for hunting, totaling in the millions. They also live in Eurasia.

32. WOOD DUCK

Wood Ducks are among the most beautiful of ducks with green crest, red eyes, and red on part of the beak, and have a white chin and face stripes. The male is iridescent with greens, purples, and blue; the female is brown with a white eye ring. They nest in woodland bodies of water and may stay year-round in Missouri. Notably laying a dozen whitish eggs in tree cavities, so that the fledglings must leap down into the water. At one time rare because of overhunting and forest clearance, they have made a comeback with the aid of suitably placed nest boxes.

33. BROWN-HEADED COWBIRD

The Brown-headed Cowbird is not an easy bird to like. The female lays its eggs in the nests of other birds. Unlike some "nest parasites," such as the Old World cuckoos, they are non-discriminating, with nests of various species used. Brown-headed Cowbird hatchlings steal food intended for the rightful nestlings which then starve to death. The four or five white eggs are each laid in different nests. Shall we say, "Do not lay all your eggs in one basket." The male is black with a brown head, and the female all gray-brown. They make squeaky gurgles or rattles. It is thought that flocks of these birds followed bison on the plains eating insects dependent on the herds and stirred up by them, and that this explains their unwillingness to settle down. When the bison disappeared, they adopted cattle as their providers and moved eastward as the forests were opened up and converted into fields and pastures. I can attest their fondness for cows and newly plowed soil by my own observations during childhood. Fortunately, not all members of the blackbird family are so unlovable or lazy. Take note of the Northern (Baltimore) Oriole which is a blackbird that makes an elaborate nest.

34. RED-WINGED BLACKBIRD

Red-winged Blackbirds are much more pleasant, pretty, and musical than the cowbirds. Red-winged Blackbirds are a fixture over most of the United States. The male is black with a showy red patch on its wings. The female looks like a large, brown-streaked sparrow. I have good photographs of both sexes, but remember puzzling for some time over recognition of the female as a Red-winged Blackbird, as these are not at all a look-alike pair. Nevertheless, the male's distinctive, one-at-time call *okerdee*, as I always renered it, woos the female who lays three to five dark-spotted blue eggs in a nest constructed carefully of grass attached to marshy vegetation in a wet border of a field. They rear more than one brood each summer. When finished with parental duties, they join flocks numbering in the thousands. Although they eat insects, the flocks are so large around populated areas as to be a health hazard.

35. COOPER'S HAWK

Cooper's Hawk belongs to the Accipiters or "true hawks," which are raptors that feed mostly on birds. This is a crow-sized bird with a long tail and short wings. It is slate gray with dark cap and barred below. The call is *cack cack cack* heard over much of the United States in deciduous forests with open meadows. It is a smaller bird than the Red-tailed Hawk standing at only 14-20 inches tall and the wings with only a 28 inch span. The four or five spotted white eggs are laid in a large nest of sticks high in a tree. The male does the hunting, providing for the female and nestlings. Accipiters are known for persistent pursuit of their avian prey through the trees and underbrush.

36. COMMON CROW

When we hear the word *crow,* we immediately think of a large black bird. Indeed, crows and ravens are large, black birds although some also have white on them. However, the family also includes the jays which are strikingly colored. The family of birds known as the Corvidae share an outstanding characteristic that makes them highly adaptable. Jays, including the familiar Blue Jay, are known for their complex behavior, such as remembering where they hide acorns for later retrieval. Other members of the family, particularly Common Crows, display purposeful behavior generally thought to occur only in higher mammals, such as the primates. The New Caledonian Crow from an Island northeast of Australia has been observed fashioning wedge-shaped tools to extract insects from holes in trees, putting them in the elite group with primates that actually fashion tools. Haven't we all heard Aesop's Fable about the Crow that dropped pebbles into the jar to raise the water level to where it could drink? And yet, oddly, scientists were skeptical until the last thirty years or so that birds show intelligence. Common Crows according to some studies can recognize individual humans and remember those that have been threatening in the past. We all recognize the crow with its large 17-21 inch height and black plumage. Its body size is used as a standard by which to compare other birds. The half dozen greenish and dark-spotted eggs are incubated in a large nest of sticks.

37. KESTREL

The Kestrel is a small falcon or "Sparrow Hawk." The male has slate-blue wings, otherwise rust-colored. Never endangered like the Peregrine, this falcon lives close to human habitations over most of the country and does us a favor by taking House Sparrows. The four or five whitish eggs are simply paced in a natural or artificial cavity. The cry is *killy killy killy*.

38. BARRED OWL

The Barred Owl is widespread over the eastern states and the forests of Canada, from Labrador west through the forests bordering the plains on the north, south through the Rocky Mountains, and down the west coast as far as California. It overlaps with the endangered Spotted Owl in the west and seems to be increasing to the detriment of the latter. The Barred Owl is slightly larger with steaked or barred sides. It is more aggressive and outcompetes the smaller owl. Furthermore, the two species are known to hybridize. The Federal Wildlife Service is now trapping and removing Barred Owls from Spotted Owl territory. From my standpoint, I am quite fond of the Barred Owl as it was the common owl where I grew up in southeastern Illinois and also by my house in Missouri. At night I often hear it saying (asking?), "who cooks for you, who cooks for you all." I occasionally see them flying in the daytime with their characteristic blunt face, and then usually mobbed by smaller birds.

39. SPOTTED SANDPIPER

Spotted Sandpipers are shore birds that nest over much of the United States and Canada, and winter in the southern states and south to South America. Spotted Sandpipers are smaller than a crow, and are brown with speckled breast and belly in summer plumage. Fall plumage in adults lacks speckles as do juveniles, leading to confusion in identification, as I know having followed and photographed one on Roaring River. I finally convincing myself that it did not have spots for a reason. It bobs its tail up and down as it looks for food at the edge of a stream or pond. The brown-spotted eggs are laid in a nest lined with grass in a depression on the ground.

40. DARK-EYED JUNCO

The Dark-eyed Junco is a frequent winter visitor to bird feeders in most of the country. Because of the birds distinctive seasonal migration to the south, hence escaping winter in the north, they are often called "snowbirds," going back at least as far as John James Audubon in the early nineteenth century. Of course, this name is also used for people who go south to leave winter behind.

They are very similar to sparrows but with a darker head and back, and a gray throat set off from the white abdomen. White is seen on the sides of the tail in flight. The beak is pink. The most common subspecies of the Dark-eyed Junco is designated as the Slate-colored Junco because of the dark gray back, resembling the smooth metamorphic rock once closely associated with the school room "chalk board." Although they flock in winter, along with other sparrows, Downy Woodpeckers, and Black-capped Chickadees, the juncos pair off in nesting season when they lay three to six brown-spotted pale green to blue eggs. The nest is not far above ground but concealed in vegetation growing on the floor of the forest. The nest is deeply concave and constructed of grass and other vegetation, or even bark that is shredded off. They eat insects in the summer, in addition to their usual fare of seeds, like millet, chickweed, and buckwheat. They search near the ground in leaf litter, and may dart upward for small insects.

41. PROTHONOTARY WARBLER

The Prothonotary Warbler lives primarily in swampy forests with large trees, and this habitat is common in Missouri, particularly in the southeastern part of the state. The male is a striking golden-orange with blue-gray on the wings and the female is similar but duller.

The song of this beautiful bird is *sweet sweet sweet.* The pair finds a tree cavity in which to build a nest, unusual for warblers, which usually nest in undergrowth. The Prothonotary Warbler is found as far north as Minnesota and south to the Gulf, but it winters in the tropics. Warblers are generally insect eaters. Apparently, the Prothonotary Warbler leaves for the winter in the fall, as the last record was 12 October 2020 in Dunklin County, and has not returned yet. Of the 100+ species of wood warblers, or Parulidae, 52 species breed in North America. The majority of them breed in northern forests and winter in the tropics, meaning that most Americans see them only in migration. In the spring, when they have breeding plumage, they are brightly colored and relatively easy to identify. However, they molt before migrating south again, giving rise to the notorious "fall warbler" problem for birders when identification hallmarks largely disappear.

42. OTHER WARBLERS

Many warblers nest in northern conifer and mixed forests where there can be considerable competition for insects, their most important food items. With many species sharing the same summer coniferous forests and, hence, potentially competing with each other, the various species feed in different specialized niches. Some hunt insects near the ground, others near the tops of trees; some look for insects close to the trunk, and others farther out in the branches. This "divide and conquer" approach to each getting its needs for life, is called "resource partitioning." A classic illustration in biology textbooks shows warblers in a conifer, each occupying a different part of the tree. An example of five such warbler species shows Black-throated Green Warbler around the middle of the tree; Yellow-rumped Warbler at the bottom of the tree; Cape May Warbler at the top of the tree; Bay-Breasted Warbler in the center of the tree; and Blackburnian Warbler at the top center of the tree. Though they do not nest in Missouri, they migrate through in the spring and fall and are listed with last date recorded in Missouri on e-bird: Black-throated Green Warbler on 1 November 2020 in St Louis County; Yellow-rumped Warbler on 2 March 2021 in Cole County; Cape May Warbler on 23 October 2020 in St. Louis County; Bay-Breasted Warbler on 12 October 2020 in Pemiscot County; and Blackburnian Warbler on 12 October 2020 in St. Louis County.

43. WILD TURKEY

Turkeys are the New World's gift to the Old World. Abundant game and vital to early Europeans, they were shipped almost immediately to Europe where they added to holiday fare, much as they do here. Turkeys are big birds. The male may stand 48 inches tall (16 pounds) and the female 36 inches (9 pounds). Both are dusky brown with black bars and a bronze-like sheen. The head is distinctive, being naked with blue and red flaps called wattles. The tail is shaped like a fan with light brown tips. The male has spurs and what resembles a beard on its chest. The female lacks these and is smaller. They gobble like domestic turkeys, but you will know the difference by the behavior. The wild ones will hear you coming and run off or, by wild beating of the wings, fly off far enough to be safe and run again. They give hunters a challenge. They can surprise you though. I was sitting quietly by the creek on campus, and I looked up to see the ugliest red, wrinkled head looking down on me, just before he fled with his hens. Turkeys were both over-hunted and deprived of the oak woodlands once so common. Both have fortunately come back in the last thirty years. They have expanded from their original eastern range into the southwest portion of the country by re-introduction.

44. WHITE-BREASTED NUTHATCH

This year-round resident of Missouri has a very distinctive call that may be described as *yank yank yank.* The bird, as expected, has a white breast and also face, but the top of the head has a black stripe and the back is an almost bluish gray. The White-breasted Nuthatch climbs usually along the trunk of a tree, often going down headfirst, gripping with one foot and leaning on the other, looking for insects to dine on. They are statewide, but I remember them most distinctly in Roaring River State Park in Barry County where one summer I camped for a week about twenty years ago. There were many large sycamore trees in the campground and oaks and other trees ascending the bluff on the other side of the river. My best photographs, however, are from a winter walk in the woods when the birds are easily visible, and there is no foliage to hide them.

45. PHEASANT

Here is an introduced gamebird popular with everyone. It was introduced from Asia, and there is no ecological equivalent in North America. It is a large chicken-like bird of grasslands, closest to grouse ecologically. However, grouse either live in forested areas in the north and east or drier areas in the west. Quail are forest edge animals and much smaller. Pheasants are very popular game birds being both challenging and tasty.

46. BOBWHITE QUAIL

Bobwhite Quail are popular game animals in the East and Midwest. They prefer fields with fencerows. As farms got bigger and row crops dominant then quail became less common. In some cases, birds have been restocked to the wild from stock raised in captivity. This is an easy bird to identify as it repeats its name frequently, "Bob White."

The birds move in groups, or "coveys," of a dozen or so through the brush and suddenly flush with cackles and a loud whir of wings, causing the inexperienced hunter to be startled and off the mark. Quail are small, chicken-like birds that are brown above, pale and streaked below, with a face that is black and white in males, or buff and white in females. Some western species of quail have crests or ornaments on the head, but not the Bobwhite Quail. The nest, hidden in grass, will serve as a place to incubate a dozen or so white eggs. The hatchlings are up and moving quickly after hatching, searching for insects to eat. Adults feed mostly on seeds and other vegetation. The quail belong to the same family as grouse, partridges, ptarmigan, partridges, pheasants, and turkeys.

47. DOWNY WOODPECKER

Without doubt I have more closeup photos of Downy Woodpeckers than any other bird. They are year-round residents but are particularly evident in the winter with no foliage to hide them as they peck for insects along the trunk and branches. When intent on looking for food, hiding is not something they take too seriously. Be a little persistent and you will get within good photo distance. Or, put up a feeder, especially with soot (fat) that they crave to keep up their highly energetic activities.

48. DOUBLE-CRESTED CORMORANT

Lewis and Clark saw many different birds on their journey in the beginning of the nineteenth century, most of which are still extant, even if not commonly seen in Missouri. They described a bird as a "loon" although it was more likely a Double-crested Cormorant which does swim with a loon-like profile. Cormorants are mostly ocean shore birds, but the Double-crested Cormorant nests in the north central U.S. and adjacent Canada in open water. The birds may be seen in Missouri on their way south to the Gulf for winter or back north in the spring or even earlier, as seen on 1 March 2021 on Blue Springs Lake in Jackson County. It is a big bird at 33 inches tall and 52 inches in wingspan, usually dark brown but lighter on the breast. During breeding season, both the male and the female sport an orange throat and beak, and either whitish or blackish plumes on the back of the head. The Cormorants, like the related Anhinga, are diving birds that feed on fish.

49. AMERICAN COOT

This could have been the bird that Lewis and Clark called a "loon" as they traveled up the Missouri River over two centuries ago. The American Coot swims low in the water like a loon. This bird is dark gray, except for a white bill protruding from a white frontal on its forehead with a touch of red at the top. American Coots are usually found in groups swimming in ponds and marshes and diving for aquatic plants or walking clumsily on land eating grass or other vegetation. They lay pink eggs with brown spots on a platform-like nest anchored in the reeds. The Coot looks like a duck but does not quack like a duck, rather it clucks, cackles, and grunts. It belongs to the rail family though larger than most and with partly webbed feet good for swimming, unlike most rails. I have photographs of a Coot from Reelfoot Lake in Tennessee that I took from a boardwalk. I started slowly walking toward it, taking pictures as I went and a last one, as I pulled abreast, but then the camera did a fast film rewind, causing my hand to shake a little, causing it to be slightly out of focus. Aren't digital cameras great!

50. GREAT BLUE HERON

Great Blue Herons nest commonly over most of the country and winter in about the southern half. Standing about four feet tall on long, spindly legs, it is easy to identify. However, they are not always blue which has caused problems in knowing what to call it. There are white forms which are distinguished by greenish-yellow legs from Great Egrets and the smaller Snowy Egret,

117

generally more southern birds. Herons are wading birds that quietly stalk fish and frogs in diverse bodies of water. Not a songster, they simply squawk. The three to seven greenish-blue eggs are laid in a stack of sticks in trees as part of a colony. Herons can be a problem in ornamental ponds where they destroy expensive varieties of coy. The trick is to place a decoy heron. When a heron flies over with its characteristically folded neck, it will see that the territory is already taken and keep on flying.

OTHER HELPFUL RESOURCES

Websites

"The Bluebird"
Link to Wikipedia -
https://en.wikipedia.org/wiki/Bluebird

"Lewis and Clark Journal: June 26, 1804"
Link to Lewis and Clark Journals -
https://lewisandclarkjournals.unl.edu/item/lc.
jrn.1804-06-26

"Ten Highlights: Birds of Missouri"
Link to Bird Watcher's Digest -
https://www.birdwatchersdigest.com/bwdsite
/explore/regions/midwest/missouri/ten-
highlights-birds-of-missouri.php

"Audubon Bird Guide"

Link to Audubon Bird Guide - https://www.audubon.org/bird-guide

"The Spotted Owl"

Link to Wikipedia - https://en.wikipedia.org/wiki/Spotted-Owl

"eBird: Missouri Birding"

Link to eBird - https://ebird.org/region/US-MO

"Owls of Harry Potter"

Link to Laura Erickson's Website - https://www.lauraerickson.com/page/owls-of-harry-potter/

Print

"Bird Brainiacs," *National Geographic*, February 2018, pp. 108-129, by Virginia Morell.

"Coherent scattering of ultraviolet light by avian feather barbs," Richard Prum, Staffan Anderrsson, and Rodolfo Torres, The Auk, vol. 120 (1), January 2003, pp. 163-170.

"Timing of Autumn Migration of Sora (*Porzana carolina*) in Missouri," Auriel Fournier, Doreen Mengel, Edward Gbur, and David Krementz, The Wilson Journal of Ornithology, vol. 129 (4), December 2017, pp. 765-770. Stable URL: https://www.jstor.org/stable/26429869.

National Audubon Society: Field Guide to North American Birds, Alfred A. Knopf, Inc., New York, 1998 by John Bull and John Farrand, Jr.

National Audubon Society: The Sibley Guide to Birds, Alfred A. Knopf, Inc., New York, 2000 by David Allen Sibley.

READ OTHER
50 THINGS TO KNOW
BOOKS

Stay up to date with new releases on Amazon: https://amzn.to/2VPNGr7

CZYKPublishing.com

www.ingramcontent.com/pod-product-compliance
Lightning Source LLC
Chambersburg PA
CBHW071023250726

48653CB00005B/1691